I0475014

Money Seeds

Seven Simple Principles to Create
Extraordinary Value

Lee Wibberding

Acknowledgments

"If you walk with the wise you will become wise."
                    – King Solomon, Proverbs 13:20

I have certainly grown *wiser* from the input of the following people. This is a better book because of them.

Milton Adams

Brian Carson

Josh Fette

Jeff Staddon

Dedication

This book is dedicated to my parents. Their love and support have molded who I am today.

Contents

Introduction..1

Part One - Understanding Value................5
Money is Not Real...7
It's About Desire..25

Part Two - Creating Value..........................37
Agreements...39
Specialization..49
Not the Way We've Always Done It...............63
Incentives..71
The Blame Game...81
Rich on $1,500 a Month.................................89
Last Thoughts...97

Introduction

In every seed lies potential. Contained within a small package is the information to turn air, water, sunlight, and nutrients into something valuable and beautiful. Without the seed these remain just what they are. Nothing changes. Nothing more valuable is created. But when the seed is planted, then what is ordinary is changed into something extraordinary. More seeds are created. Life happens and the world changes.

Imagine we found seeds that grow money. Would you plant them? Would you water and care for their growth? Would you harvest some seeds from the plant and grow some more?

I don't have physical seeds. There is no coupon in the back of this book to send away for your own.

But I can offer you thought seeds. They do the same thing. They contain information that will allow you to create something valuable out of scarce resources. They explain the basics of economics and how money **really** works.

In the world of economics things can get complicated. An ocean of information is all around us. You can learn almost anything you want. But with so much out there, how do you know what is worth knowing and what is just a distraction that will pull you under the waves?

Five years ago I didn't know. I was swimming like everyone else, trying to make sense of it all. I had dabbled in the stock market, losing several hundred dollars. Since that didn't work I tried satisfying my need for sophistication by trading stock options (think trading stock insurance). It was still a losing effort. Next I tried real estate. One foreclosure later I learned I don't prefer being a land lord anyway. It became clear I was making my finances worse, not better.

During this time of consistent failure, a friend suggested if someone studies a subject for fifteen minutes a day, they will be an expert in a few years. Considering my efforts so far were poor, I thought the study of economics may be worth a try.

So a journey began that has culminated in this short book. I read everything I could on the subject. From modern material all the way back to Adam Smith's four volume set *On the Wealth of Nations* written in 1776. The goal of my journey was to make sense of what matters in business and what doesn't. Then I could use my new found skills to be a successful business person.

To my surprise, it actually works. There are a few principles that explain everything. They are profound, yet simple. Like seeds, they give you the information you need to create value.

The goal of this book is to give you a framework to understand economics. When you understand the principles, everything falls together in a nice organized way. The ocean of information turns into a sensible structure.

Although hundreds of pages could be written on the subject, the goal is to make it simple. So I have endeavored to make this book as short as possible while still explaining each concept.

Welcome to the journey . . .

Part One

Understanding Value

Money is Not Real

---

*"I have enough money to last me
the rest of my life, unless
I buy something."*
Jackie Mason
1880-1956

So it turns out money is not real. That's hard to think about because we use it so much. I buy real groceries with money. I put real gas in my tank to drive down a real road. I buy real wood to build a shed. But money itself is not real.

In a large economy like the United States, it's difficult to see how money really works. There are millions of people interrelating every hour of each day. It can feel very complicated. So to say money is not real becomes hard to prove unless we consider something very basic.

So let's consider the simplest economy. Maybe by looking at the small we can understand the large.

We find ourselves looking in on a beautiful tropical island with four people. There is a builder who repairs huts and builds anything else needed. There is a farmer who grows food. A clothes maker makes clothes, and a fisherman catches fish to supplement the farmer's produce. Four people, four skills. We have an economy.

Fisherman

Builder

Clothes Maker

Farmer

As we observe we notice the islanders have developed a trading system with rare shells they found on the island. It works like this.

1. The farmer needs his roof repaired on his hut. He gives the builder a shell to do the job.

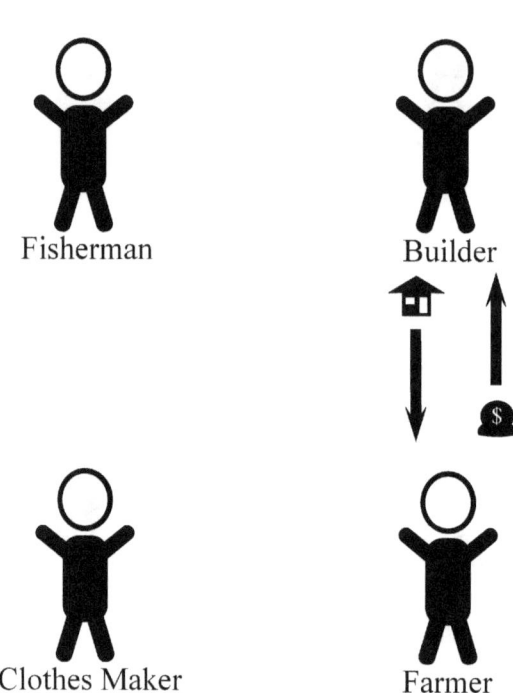

Fisherman

Builder

Clothes Maker

Farmer

2. The builder is hungry. He takes the shell the farmer gave him and buys a fish from the fisherman.

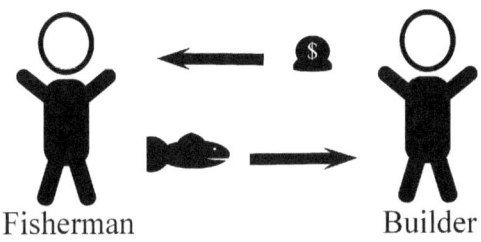

Fisherman   Builder

Clothes Maker   Farmer

3. The fisherman needs a new shirt, so he takes the shell the builder gave him and gives it to the clothes maker for the shirt.

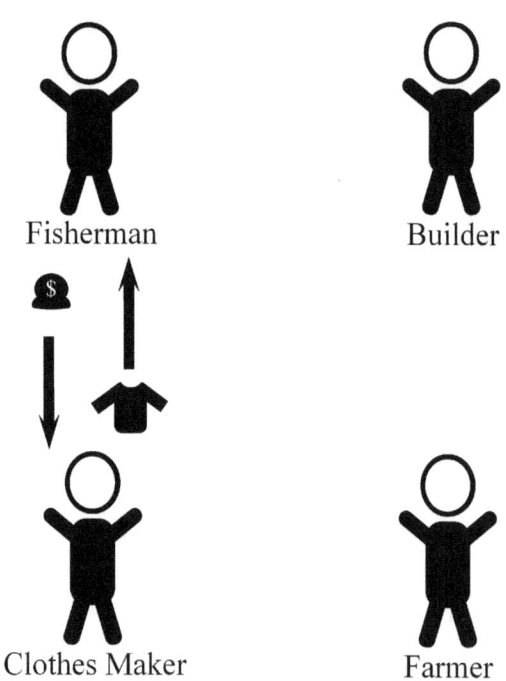

Fisherman

Builder

Clothes Maker

Farmer

4. The clothes maker is hungry, so trades the shell to the farmer for some potatoes.

Fisherman   Builder

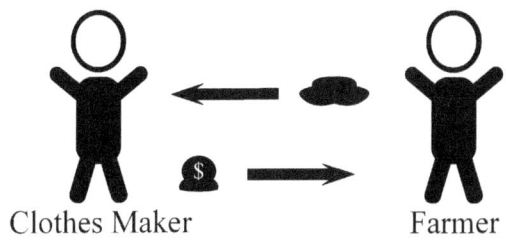

Clothes Maker   Farmer

Notice what happens here. There is only one shell. Go back and look. As that one shell passes from person to person it enables all four people to get the stuff they want. The farmer has the same shell he starts with, but a lot of trade happens. Four people have stuff they want, but the money situation (or shells in this case) is exactly the same. Money is used to allow the trades to happen, but the farmer still ends up with the same shell he had at the start.

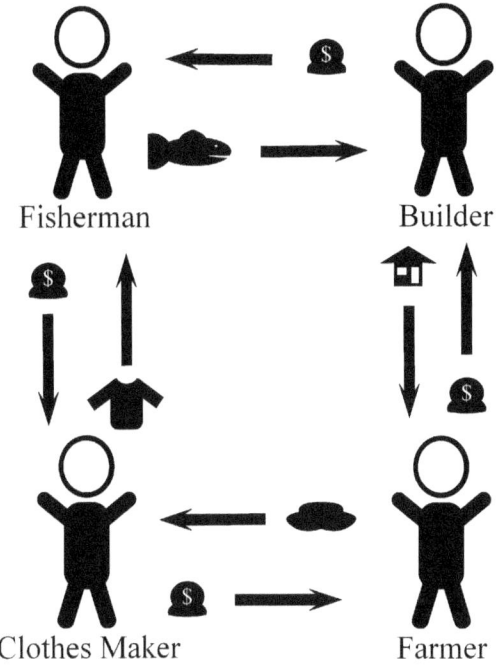

It doesn't matter if the "currency" happens to be a shell or a dollar. The islanders could have used a twenty dollar bill to do the trading rather than the shell.

The key point here is this: The shell is not what

is valuable. It works as a *point system* to allow valuable products and services to be traded. In a sense it is **not real** because it holds no real value.

This becomes clear if we send a financial disaster to the island. One night the wind blows all night and in the morning there are thousands of shells washed up on the beach.

Our islander friends are happy. They are rich! The fisherman walks the beach all day collecting shells. So do the rest. By the end of the day every hut is packed full of shells. The good times have come. No more working hard just to survive because everyone is rich.

The next day the clothes maker is getting ready to make clothes, but then asks herself, *why*? She has all the money she needs for years to come. Why not sit back and relax? So instead of setting up the loom, she heads down to the beach to buy a fish for breakfast – possibly two. After all, she is a rich woman.

The docks are empty. The fisherman is not selling fish today. She walks over to the farmers house, but there is nothing for sale. Even the builder is not building. Everyone has plenty of money, but nothing to buy because no one is creating valuable products or services to trade. The money is worthless.

Money is not real. It is merely a point system to determine who is owed value. The true source of wealth is in the valuable products or services that are created.

Which brings us to the first principle of economics:

Principle 1

Wealth comes from creating value

Every economy in the world is based on businesses creating value. Each business has their unique way of doing this, but if we follow it back to it's source, all wealth comes from creating value somewhere. Always.

Sometimes governments try to increase value by printing more money. But it doesn't work because wealth comes from creating value. When more money is pumped into an economy it merely spreads out the value over more dollars, so each dollar is worth less.

Sometimes this can get really crazy. Between 2004 and 2008 the country of Zimbabwe started on a money creation spree. By the time it ended in the total collapse of the Zimbabwe currency they were printing single bills of $100,000,000,000,000 (a hundred trillion) Zimbabwe dollars! That sounds great until you realize that it took hundreds of billions of Zimbabwe dollars to equal the value of a single US dollar.

There are only two factors that determine the long term value of money:

1. How much money is in the economy

2. The amount of value in products or services created in a specific time frame.

This is it. Governments may increase the money supply to try to stimulate spending so we will create more value, but printing money in itself never produces value.

Summary

This principle is the foundation of all economics. Pause before you go on and think about the idea of wealth existing from creating value. Make a list of businesses in your town that have both succeeded and failed. Ask the question, *How does this business create value?* For the failed businesses ask, *How did this business fail to create enough value to survive?*

Planting

Seeds don't do anything unless they are planted. It's time to put these ideas into real life situations. Through the rest of this book we will follow two people who are each starting their own business to see how they can apply these principles.

Jack decides to start a bakery. He enjoys baking and is good at what he does. Jennifer chooses to start a cleaning business. She knows how to do this and believes she can create value by providing this service.

How can Jack create value with a bakery?

Where is Jennifer providing value?

Possible Answers

Jack provides value by making cakes, doughnuts, and breads people want. He can also make other products. He will be rewarded with more customers, more consistent customers, or bigger profits the more value he can provide.

Jennifer provides value through the service of cleaning. People find it more valuable to have a clean house than a dirty one. Businesses find it more valuable to have a clean workplace than a dirty one.

Personal Success Questions

How do you use this principle for personal success? Stop thinking about money and start thinking about value. Ask yourself, "How can I create value in my life and business?" If you think about it in this way, new possibilities will open. Thinking about money narrows the mind. Think about creating value.

My Plan

It's About Desire

"If you buy a $28,000 car, in four years it will be worth about 11,000 bucks.
Dave Ramsey

Where does value come from? We know wealth comes from creating value. But what is value? When a stock loses value does the value hide somewhere only to spring up another place in the economy? What about products like crude oil that was once an annoying black goo no one wanted. Now it's a multi-billion dollar industry. Where did all that value come from?

Although it seems counter-intuitive, there is no limit to how much value exists on the earth at one time. Huge amounts are created and lost every day.

Because . . .

Principle 2

Value is created in the human mind

Every kind of value is explained by understanding someone on earth wants it.

If no one lived on earth, what would be valuable? Gold, money, businesses – nothing. Because all value is traced back to the fact that some human wants it. This, coupled with the idea that wealth comes from creating value builds the twin foundation of all economics. These two principles lay the groundwork for everything else. The rest of this book is about building on this foundation.

This principle goes further than just laying a foundation. It also explains three other ideas that reveal how to create exceptional value.

Value

Someone
creates it

Someone
wants it

First, it helps us find how likely the value of a product or service will change. Second, it helps us understand supply and demand, a major concept of business. Last, it explains how advertising works.

Stability of Value

Since value is created in the human mind, stable value depends on how likely people will change their mind. If people continue to want it, it will continue to be valuable. If not, it will lose it's value. In the mid 1990's a small stuffed animal filled with little plastic pellets became enormously popular as a toy and collectible. In a few years the Beanie Baby fad faded, wiping out millions of dollars in "value". In much the same way the price of stocks move up and down based on the combined whims of thousands of people. People change their minds and with it the value of things change.

A Psychologist named Abraham Maslow helps us here. He developed a hierarchy of needs which begins to explain the choices people make about what is valuable. He suggests people don't care much about needs higher on the chart if the basic needs are not met. For example, if I am running for my life (which means I don't feel safe), I don't care too much about food. If I am hungry, I'm not thinking about friendship.

The more basic a human need you are fulfilling with your product or service, the more stable it will be in value. A person who opens a grocery store can expect her sales to be more stable than the one who is selling the latest fad in clothing. Fad clothing may be a good business, but expect what was hot yesterday may not sell today.

Supply and Demand

Humans create value. But we don't all value the same products in the same way. One may be willing to pay $1.50 for a big juicy apple. Another likes bananas more and would only pay a dollar for the apple. Value is human and value is personal. We should expect differences.

Imagine seven people lined up according to how much they would pay for an apple.

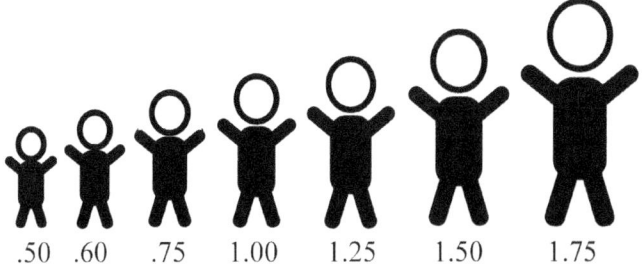

.50   .60   .75   1.00   1.25   1.50   1.75

If I sell apples for $1.50 how many people will buy? How about $.75?

By understanding that different people place different value on the same product, we begin to understand the concept of supply and demand. People don't line up in the neat line in real life, but they are out there and each has their idea of the worth of the apple. By setting a price for your apple, you have an opportunity to make a sale to all those who value an apple more than the price you set.

Advertising

As a seller of apples wouldn't it be great if you could change the mind of those seven people? If you could find a way to help each person value an apple just fifty cents more, you could raise the price and make more money. It turns out you can.

Advertising not only spreads the message about a product or service, it can also change the way we think. If advertising changes the way we value something, because value is created in the mind, it actually changes its value.

By seeing images of products that make us feel good, or give a laugh, the perception of that product changes in our minds. Businesses not only create value when they perform their service, but also create value in the way the service is presented.

Advertising creates value in a very real way because value is created in the human mind and advertising influences the mind.

Summary

Understanding value is created in the human mind and wealth come from creating value are the foundation of all economics. If you quit reading right now, you can understand any economy on earth just by asking, *Where is the value created?* and *Why do the people value what they do?* It takes some digging, but any economy will open up if you keep asking these two questions as you work through the layers.

Planting

After reading this chapter:

What can Jack do to increase the value of his baked goods?

What can Jennifer do to increase the value of her cleaning service?

Possible Answers

Although there are hundreds of ways to increase value, here are a few ideas.

Jack could:

- Create sample platters to allow customers to try more of his breads, providing a way to increase their value in the customer's mind.

- Bring his bakery to potential customer's minds by advertising on the radio.

Jennifer could:

- Provide convenient cleaning hours after businesses close.

- Make a flyer for her clients to show the psychological benefits of a clean house.

Personal Success Questions

1. Stability – How likely will people continue to want my product or service?

2. Added Value – How can I add value to my product or service by the way I present it?

My Plan

Part Two

Creating Value

Agreements

Agreements are a major source of value creation. An agreement brings together resources from more than one person to create more value than can be created separately. Which brings us to the next principle.

Principle 3

Add value by creating agreements

Here's how it works. You decide to hire someone to build a deck. A builder is located and he comes out to your house to give an estimate. What will determine whether or not you will hire him?

Each one of you has a point where it doesn't make sense to enter an agreement. The builder can only bid so low until he won't make any money. You also have a limit to how much you are willing to pay. At some point you will decide a deck is not worth it, or go with another builder.

These "break even" points will determine how much value is created in the deal. Often in business this is called a BATNA, or Best Alternative To Negotiated Agreement. Just a big word meaning your break even point, or the point at which it doesn't make sense to enter an agreement.

For purpose of example let's assume your break even point is five hundred dollars. If the deck builder charges more than five hundred dollars it makes more sense to go with another builder, or choose not to build the deck.

Considering time and materials, let's say the builder is better off spending his time somewhere else if you offer him anything less than two hundred dollars.

$200
Builder's
BATNA

$500
Your
BATNA

Between these two points is where value is created in any agreement. An agreement creates value because each person is better off. They have more value by entering it rather than not.

In this case three hundred dollars worth of value is created (the difference between two and five hundred).

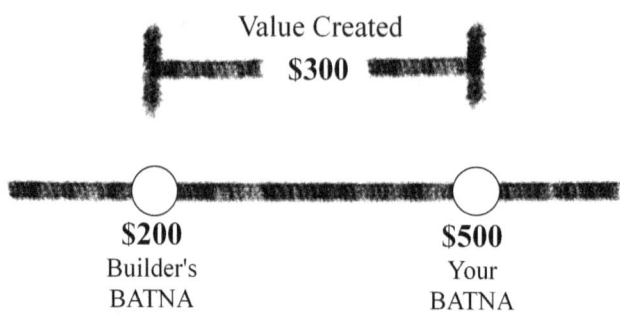

Negotiation

Determining who gets the value is the realm of negotiation. If the agreed on price for the deck is $350, then each party will get $150 of value they didn't have before.

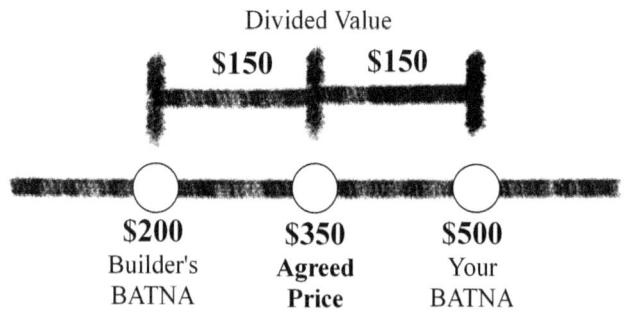

If the agreement is $300, you will get $200 of value and the builder $100.

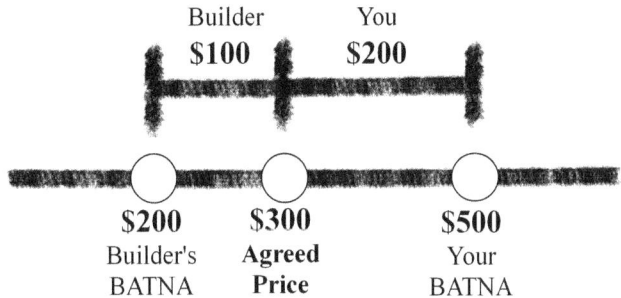

At times it is tempting to do everything yourself. However, agreements create environments where each person is better off by entering an agreement than trying to do everything themselves. The next principle will expand on this idea.

Planting

Jennifer's business is booming. She is working sixty to eighty plus hours a week just to keep up with her client's cleaning needs.

How can Jennifer use the principle of agreements to slow down?

Jack has been thinking about buying frozen dough from a vendor. Currently it takes him on average 5 minutes to make a loaf of bread. Buying frozen dough would bring this down to 3 minutes. But Jack is worried because due to the higher cost from the vendor he would only make a profit of $2.50 per loaf instead of $3.00.

What advice would you give Jack?

Possible Answers

It's time for Jennifer to hire employees. Most likely she will be able to charge the clients more than the employees cost her. Although it's tempting to grasp all the work in her hands, by hiring employees she can take in more business and actually make more money than trying to do everything herself.

Jack makes twelves loaves an hour right now. At three dollars a piece he makes $36 an hour[1]. If he buys dough from the vendor he will only make $2.50 per loaf. But this will allow him to make twenty loaves in an hour, or $50 an hour[2]. It's time for Jack to use the power of agreements to create more value.

---

1   12 loaves x $3.00 each.
2   20 loaves x $2.50 each.

Personal Success Questions

1. What am I doing right now that could be better handled by an agreement?

2. In every negotiation ask: Where is my break even point? Where is the other parties break even point? Between these two points is the value created.

My Plan

Specialization

Once we understand the way value is created by agreements, it opens the way for specialization. You may have noticed people who go to school for a long time tend to make more money. One of the reasons for this is how few of them there are compared to the population. This rarity increases their value by weeding out the competition. However, there is more going on than just rare skills. By specializing, more value is created than being a jack of all trades.

When I need a brain surgeon, I want the best. I may be able to hire a doctor who has a 70% success rate for a tenth of the cost of the one with a 95% success rate. I'm all for a bargain, but in this case the one with the higher success rate is much more valuable to me. The value of doing it right makes up for any discounts.

This is also true for any other profession. A person who is better at what they do creates more value – often substantially more. So in any industry you will almost always create more value by being really good at one or two skills and letting others do the rest. Which brings us to the next principle.

Principle 4
Specialize to multiply value

By letting alone those things you don't do best, you will free up time and money to do those things you do best. Because we can use agreements to trade services, it makes us all better off. This is what economists call *Comparative Advantage.*

It is a little counter-intuitive because it often seems I will be better off doing everything myself. But notice how it works.

Bob and Amy Set Up Shop

Bob decides to set up shop in Anywhere City, USA. Bob likes to make candles and soap, so he establishes his store front, hires a sales person and begins spending his days making soap and candles to sell in the front of his store.

By chance, Amy also starts a store across town selling soap and candles. She too hires a sales person and spends her days in the back room making soap and candles to sell in her store.

Bob soon finds he can make five bars of soap in

an hour, or he can make ten candles in an hour. He decides to divide up his time and spend four hours a day making soap and four making candles. Here are the results:

Bob's Workday

Person	Hours	Soap	Candles
Bob	4	20	
Bob	4		40
Total	**8**	**20**	**40**

Amy is a lot better than Bob at soap making. She can make twenty bars in an hour. She is just as skilled as Bob at candle making. Since her customer's want both she too divides her time between the jobs:

Amy's Workday

Person	Hours	Soap	Candles
Amy	4	80	
Amy	4		40
Total	**8**	**80**	**40**

Notice between the two shops there are a hundred soaps and eighty candles made in a day.

Both Combined

Person	Hours	Soap	Candles
Bob	8	20	40
Amy	8	80	40
Total	**16**	**100**	**80**

One day the two are talking. Bob is amazed at how much better Amy is at soap making. He is not too good at math, but senses there is something here he could benefit from. He suggests to Amy that he make all the candles for both shops and she make all the soap. She doesn't think she would gain much from the trade since she is just as good as Bob at candle making. But because Bob asked nicely she decides to try it for a day. After all, it might be nice to just concentrate on soap.

At the end of the day Bob has made eighty candles. Amy has made a hundred a sixty soaps.

Shared Workday

Person	Hours	Soap	Candles
Bob	8	0	80
Amy	8	160	0
Total	**16**	**160**	**80**

Bob keeps forty candles and takes forty over to Amy. Amy keeps her usual eighty soaps, gives Bob twenty (which is what he usually makes in a day).

They both notice there are sixty extra soaps, which they decide to split.

Split

Person	Soap	Candles
Bob	20	40
Amy	80	40
Extra	60	0
Total	**160**	**80**

What happened?

Amy was freed up to do what she does best – make soap. It may have seemed like Amy wouldn't benefit from the trade. However, what it allowed her to do it free up time to create more value. She created more value because she could concentrate on soap and didn't have to spend time making candles.

The same happened for Bob. Even though he

wasn't really good at either, Bob was able to concentrate on what he did best and provide for his soap making needs in another, less time demanding way.

This is why specialization is so powerful. By using the power of agreements described in the previous chapter, Amy and Bob can now specialize. Since we can create agreements, we can specialize. All our other needs can be taken care of by trade. If we create value by doing what we do best, then trade, everyone is better off. For Amy and Bob it meant sixty extra bars of soap magically appear.

Planting

Jennifer is cleaning businesses, and homes. She has hired employees, but still feels she can focus her efforts more. She makes more money cleaning businesses than homes.

How could Jennifer use the principle of specialization?

Jack makes cakes, doughnuts, and bread. Cakes make good money but interrupt the work flow of everything else going on. There are a few customers who order doughnuts, but most get theirs at the coffee shop next door. Bread is where he makes money most consistently.

How can Jack use the principle of specialization?

Possible Answers

Jennifer decides to specialize in just cleaning businesses. Since she has dropped the house cleaning, she finds it takes her half the time to train employees since they are only trained for one kind of cleaning. Since she cleans businesses in the evening it frees up her afternoons to look for more clients. With more business she can hire more employees and expand her enterprise.

Jack decides to continue to provide cakes, but have them made by another shop. This allows him to still make some profit, but he doesn't have to stop everything else to do it. Doughnuts take so much time and so few people buy them he drops them all together. Remembering the prinicple of agreements he and the coffee shop agree to hand out each others coupons to expand both their business's customer base.

Dropping cakes and doughnuts from his list frees up space. Jack buys another oven and finds he can make a loaf in an average of two minutes time. Now he's up to $75 per hour[3].

---

3   30 loaves an hour x $2.50 per loaf.

Personal Success Questions

1. When it comes to creating value, what do I do best?

2. What skills can I improve to be even better at what I do best?

My Plan

Not the Way We've Always Done It

"Inventions reached their limit long ago, and I see no hope for further development"
Julius Frontinus
1ˢᵗ century A.D.

If agreements add value and specialization multiplies value, technology creates exponential value. So . . .

Principle 5

Technology creates exponential value

If you want to build wealth quickly, use technology. It is the most powerful tool we will cover in this book.

What do we mean by technology? Often we think of electronics or computers or the internet. These are big producers of value, but technology goes beyond these.

Technology is the "know-how" to put in less and get more, whatever form that takes.

Some time in history the wheel was invented. This was (and still is) valuable technology. With it humans could now create things like carts to pull behind their animals. Instead of carrying the load, it could be put in a cart, requiring less energy to carry the same load. This is the amazing effect of technology. It allows us to create more value for less effort.

Astonishing Value

The wheel may be nice, but when technology really comes into its own is when two or more come together.

What if we add some more tech to our wheel? Someone invents an air-filled tire. Suddenly our wheel also provides a smoother ride, reducing wear on the vehicle and those riding in it.

If we add the technology to distill crude oil, we can make a powerful explosive. What if we can contain the explosion in a box that drove our wheel? By adding technologies together we get something so powerful it revolutionizes transportation.

The secret to creating extreme value is by bringing technologies together to create a system that makes a mind-boggling amount of value for a small input. In this case it's an automobile.

A person can work for a day at a minimum wage job and earn enough money for the fuel to drive their car over five hundred miles. They can also make the trip in a day. A few generations ago the same trip would take twenty days and cost many times as much in time and money. Technology creates more value for less input.

It doesn't have to be a car or computer, or anything newsworthy. Anything we do to make a system that takes less and makes more is technology.

Summary

We are still building on the same foundation that wealth comes from creating value, and value is created in the human mind. Now that we've discovered the power of multiple technologies, we know how to do that very well. The basics have not changed. But we have some exceptional tools to think about new ways to create value.

Planting

Jack is has just learned about the principle of technology. He is trying to figure out how to produce more for less input.

What would you do if you were Jack?

Jennifer also wants to use technology to her advantage.

What would you do if you were Jennifer?

Possible Answers

Jack finds a faster oven and proof box. They cost more, but he believes it will cut down his costs substantially. He also decides to use a better bag which appeals to his customers. He is able to raise the price a quarter to $2.75.

With the new oven and proof box he can now make a loaf on average every 1 minute. This means $165 per hour[4].

Jennifer sets up a website where her clients can schedule her services. She also gets her workers mobile devices to check in for each job. This way more can get done in less time, which leaves Jennifer more time to makes sales.

---

4   60 loaves x $2.75

Personal Success Questions

1. How can I use technology to create more value for less input?

2. Is there new technology I can invent to create more value, either by providing more output, or less input?

3. What technologies can I combine to gain even more value?

My Plan

Incentives

---

*"Money was never a big motivation for
me, except as a way to keep score.
The real excitement is playing the game."*
Donald Trump

Have you ever made an agreement with someone only to have them not fulfill their side of the bargain? Doesn't feel so good, especially if you've bent over backwards to make sure it is a win/win for everybody. The other party failing to live up to their agreement has cost me tens of thousands of dollars. So if you can learn here rather than with your wallet, this chapter should be worth that much to you.

I like to live life without being suspicious of everyone. Most people seem nice enough and I want to keep it that way. So how do we make sure people follow through on their agreements without treating everyone like criminals waiting to happen?

The key is to build the right incentives into each agreement. This keeps the honest, honest and makes the dishonest think twice before trying to rip us off.

Principle 6

Get the incentives right to maximize value

Most people have the best intentions. But making sure it will hurt if they don't follow through and are rewarded for following through will encourage everyone to make the right decision in that moment when it matters.

Getting the incentives right really comes down to answering two questions well.

The first question is, **What is valuable to**

them?

Finding what is valuable to the other party is the first step to getting the incentives right. What is valuable to them become their incentives for entering the agreement. Although there may be others, look in these three areas.

- **Timing.** Are there products or services they need by a certain time? What if these are delivered early, is that a plus?

- **Money.** A big motivator in most agreements. When will payments be made? Can payment amounts be changed depending on performance?

- **Relationship.** How much do they value their relationship with you? Is this a one time deal, or do they have incentive to stay on good terms?

The second question to ask in every agreement is, **How can I deliver what is valuable to them**

only when I receive what I need?

Once it is clear what is valuable to the other side you can determine how to structure the agreement. A great way to do this is incrementally. Once they fulfill part of the agreement, you fulfill part of your side. A great agreement will leave no place where either side can exit without hurting. Although it is not possible to achieve this perfectly in every situation, the closer the better.

This is really simple, but it is amazing how many agreements are made with no *incentive* to follow through.

Summary

A major cause of the United States winning the Cold War with the U.S.S.R is the principle of incentives. When a worker is paid the same whether he produces a lot of value or a little, there is not a lot of incentive to produce extra value. The United

States literally created more value than the U.S.S.R. because capitalism creates better incentives than communism.

If you think about the difference the idea of incentives made during the Cold War, I guess this chapter is worth billions. How is that for under promising and over delivering?

Planting

One of Jennifer's clients never pays her on time. She's asked for prompt payment but never gets a response.

Thinking about incentives, what could Jennifer do to encourage the client to be on time?

Jack is having trouble motivating his employees to give their best effort. He is sure they could work 50% faster if they had the right motivation.

What would you suggest Jack do to motivate his employees?

Possible Solutions

Jennifer could drop the client if they are too much trouble and find another one. However, it may be less work to find incentives to motivate the current client to pay on time. A discount for on time payment, or charge for late payment would be a good place to start. Another solution would be to require a pre-payment.

Jack's situation is tricky. He could pay his employees by the loaf rather than by the hour. However, there is the risk of cutting corners and losing quality. Keeping the hourly wage, plus adding a monthly bonus based on a percentage of the profits may give the employees *ownership* of the business and motivate them to give better efforts.

Personal Success Questions

1. How can I create better incentives for those I have agreements with?

    A Employees?

    B. Customers?

    C. Vendors?

My Plan

The Blame Game

*"It's not whether you win or lose,
it's how you place the blame."*
Oscar Wilde

We've come to the last principle. Whether it's a multi-billion dollar company, or a lemonade stand, you know the basics to any business and any economy.

Wealth always comes from producing value. It doesn't matter how much money is printed or where you are. Wealth is always created in the human mind. The choice of people whether they want a product or service will always determine its value. Agreements will always create value when made with wisdom. Specialization will give a person more value to trade regardless of their skill level. Technology will always give the ability to create more value with less effort – that's why it's technology. Getting the incentives right will always make better agreements.

These are the basic building blocks of any economy. They will never change and those who learn them will be better off for the effort. But there is a certain mystery we need to explain before our study is complete.

There are people who know many of these principles, and some know them all, but are not successful. Why? The principles are timeless. Over two hundred years ago Adam Smith wrote about most of them. We have hundreds of years of history that show they work. Why don't they work for some people?

I was remodeling a rental property when that eureka moment came. The reason many don't succeed is their unwillingness to grow. It takes hard work to put these into practice. What separates those who are successful is their willingness to grow. Growing is painful, hard work. But once someone knows the principles, the choice to grow is the difference between success and failure. That's why . . .

Principle 7

The number one inhibitor of wealth creation is the blame game

As part of the human race we have this part of us called self-esteem. In a very real way we feel pain when we don't think much of ourselves. So we try to avoid pain. We develop ways to protect ourselves against the pain of thinking less of who we are.

To avoid this pain of low self-worth, we tend to blame others for our problems. In the human mind this helps, because if it's not my fault then I am not a failure. Bad things just happen to me. This kind of thinking helps us feel better about ourselves (although it doesn't help those we blame), but it stops us from growing into the people we want to be. It only masks over our problems by blaming everyone else for them.

Yet, the ability to identify a problem is the first step to fixing it. To be successful requires the willingness to go through the real pain of self-evaluation and grow into a better person. We are all on a journey. No one is perfect. But our choices determine whether we are improving ourselves, or blaming others for the bad things that happen.

Getting Past the Blame

So how do you get past the blame game? It's not helpful to turn yourself into a human punching bag of blame.

When faced with a situation two questions are

helpful to process it in a healthy way.

1. What part of this situation is my fault?

You don't have to take it all to own up to your contribution. Usually there is more than one party involved. When things turn out bad, rather than passing the blame ask, *What part of this is my fault?* Own up, say you're sorry and move on. No use denying or dragging it out. It's not worth the energy.

2. Even if it's not my fault, what can I do to make it better?

Notice you are not trying to find someone else to blame. That kind of thinking just drags us down. Rather, looking for a solution leads us past the blame stage. And it reminds us we don't have to blame others to feel good. Proactively being a part of the solution is something to be proud of and should be a self-esteem boost in itself.

Summary

These two questions provide an atmosphere for you to grow. If you are willing to ask them, they will give you the power to get past some of the stuff holding you back and allow you to make these seven principles your own.

Personal Success Questions

1. In what situations do I need to stop blaming others?

2. How can I focus on growth rather than blame?

My Plan

Rich on $1,500 a Month

---

*These individuals have riches just as
we say that we "have a fever" when
really the fever has us.*
Seneca

What does it mean to be rich? Do you have to
be a millionaire? A multimillionaire? Where is the
line?

Most people seek wealth for freedom or secur-
ity. They want to make sure everything is taken
care of, and to have the time to do what they want.
These are worthy goals. The problem is that list of
"everything to take care of" gets longer and longer.
How much is enough?

Could it be the things we have, not only fail to

bring us freedom, but contribute to the bondage? We work hard to have things which we believe will bring us pleasure. Instead they drag us deeper in debt and lose their luster. The freedom we look for vanishes.

In a very real way rich is a state of mind. The older I get, the more value I place on the simple things of life. Good friends, family, paid bills, my Christian faith.

How much is enough? If a family has all their debts paid, how much do they really need to live on?

Recently I made a budget to find the minimum my family of four could reasonably live on. Although there are those who can comfortably live on less, here is what I came up with.

My Budget

Food	$400
Rent	$400
Electric	$100
Water/Sewer	$50
Gasoline	$100
Insurance	$100
Misc	$100
Emergency Savings	$250
Total	**$1,500**

Would I like to live like this for long periods of time? Not necessarily. But I could. This scenario doesn't make me feel rich – at first.

What if choosing it means I don't have to work forty to sixty hours a week or at all, but can have free time to pursue the life I want? Now I start to feel rich.

Rich is not about how much you have, but about freedom to enjoy the simple things. Even on a low income, as long as it covers expenses and you don't have to work, you are independently wealthy. If you can do it on five hundred or a thousand, you've still made it. It doesn't mean you can't work. It just means the minimum is cared for, which gives you freedom!

Summary

Learning how economics work has been freeing to me, and I imagine when ideas clicked along the way it was for you too. Once you know it begins to put the world in perspective. I know how to get it, but how much do I really want? Enough to take care of my family and do some good in the world, but after that . . .

When you know wealth comes from producing value, and value is created in the human mind, the appeal of working sixty to eighty hours a week to gain something that changes value when people change their minds is diminishing. It just doesn't call to me anymore. There are more important things in life.

Personal Success Questions

1.   Do I want freedom or possessions?

2.   If I want freedom, where can I cut my life-style to obtain it?

3.   How can I create a system of value creation that will pay for my minimum lifestyle?

My Plan

Last Thoughts

Thanks for reading this book. I hope it has opened up new understanding about how the world works.

If you start a new business or improve your life in some way as a result of these principles, I'd love to hear from you. Drop me an email and tell me about it.

Also, if you would like to learn more, I occasionally teach a class on the topic live or by webinar. To be notified when the next one is, drop by our website and sign up.

www.MyMoneySeeds.com
Email: Lee@MyMoneySeeds.com

Planning Space

The following pages are for you. It's easy to read a book. The difference happens when you apply the principles. Take some time to sketch out your own journey. Write down a step by step plan. You've answered the questions at the end of each chapter. Review them. Modify what you need to and be intentional about your future. It starts right here.

Notes

Notes

Notes

Notes

Notes

Notes

Notes

Notes

Notes

Notes

Notes